POLISH YOUR CROWN

HANDLING BUSINESS FEAR

BE DIFFERENT

BE BETTER

BE SUCCESSFUL

YOU KNOW YOU CAN!

By Ken Lord

Copyright 2018

Publisher

Kenniston W. Lord, Jr.

Syracuse, NY

ISBN 10: 1720658412

ISBN-13: 978-1720658412

WHY THIS BOOK

Throughout my career, I have written extensively about motivation, ambition, objectives, attitude, performance, and the all-out fear of failure I've witnessed in business. In sixty years, I've witnessed a lot of it.

For most of my career, I have focused on teaching and writing not only about the "why" of an effort but also about the "how" that the effort requires.

During the last major effort of my career, I ran several Avon retail stores and conducted business in six figures. I learned a lot about success during that.

That led me to write a narrative nonfiction, somewhat like a small novel, that led a new representative through all the pangs of the birth of a small Avon business and through the decision-making processes to make that business large and successful. That particular story was published under several titles, the most recent being THE RELUCTANT AVON LADY.

As I did so, I worked also on this, a purely nonfiction set of guidelines designed to work on any platform, not exclusively Avon. I invite you to read it.

Enjoy

Ken Lord
Syracuse, NY

Ken Lord

.

CONTENTS

PREFACE

What makes a person successful?

Is it, as some would have you to believe, as simple as being born of successful parents? For some it has been. For most, it has not. Sometimes the offspring of successful people are anything but successful themselves. Often successful people are successful precisely because they were *not* born into success and have seen that for them to be equally successful, they must expend extraordinary efforts.

Is it merely the coincidence of being in the right place at the right time? Good fortune comes to those who are prepared for it.

Is it *the luck of the draw*, as some lottery winners would have you to believe? Perhaps, but it can be well demonstrated that your odds of hitting the lottery are about the same as being hit by lightning.

Is it strictly *"location, location, location,"* as the real estate people would tell you? Real estate people sell property in any location that produces a commission.

Should you cross your fingers or read your horoscope daily? It's good for a laugh, but don't live your life by it.

"Carpe Diem," said Robin Williams in *The Dead Poet's Society*. "Seize the day." SIEZE THE DAY! Grab it and shake it with intensity. Attack it with passion. Accept nothing but the best. Second best is not good enough.

The steps for success in business are the same for success of any endeavor you may undertake. Whatever is worth doing is worth doing well.

A worthy activity pushes some attribute of your life forward. If your interests are intellectual, then find ways to improve skills, develop your mind, or satisfying your need of accomplishment. It is a worthy purpose of living. Or it may be the improvement of relations, an improvement to your financial health, or an advance of your intellect or your security. It may be the recognition of your achievements.

Whatever it turns out to be, it involves a *change* from *before* to *after*. Thus, a specific plan will be needed. The degree and severity of change will determine the schedule and the activities. It will consume the degree of passion needed by your efforts.

Carefully distinguish between things that happen naturally and those efforts that, if properly invested, can *push* the accomplishment along. Consider: "Things worth doing well are equally worth doing quickly."

That holds for most things other than concrete and culinary art.

For everything that has a natural delay, some tasks can be accelerated. In business, compounding is a slow and progressive increase in the worth of an asset. The aggressive investment of such assets derives the greatest return in the shortest time. While that may be true, it isn't true in every case. For some, the risk is simply too high or the reward is simply too low or too far away.

Some say going fast promotes error. That may be true. But how important? Except for safety concerns, every error is reversible, recoverable, or repeatable.

Those who are passionate about something are in a hurry to achieve success. You don't need to jump into the deep end to see if you can swim. You don't need to expose yourself to foolish danger. It does mean that more extensive planning, more extensive data gathering, and a more thorough use of resources will be necessary. Deadlines set a firm endpoint; the role of passion is to make a deadline unnecessary.

Eventually someone will suggest that sacrifice is needed. It's true. Time is a finite resource. It will take effort. The more effort given to one thing means less to another. The economist calls this a *production possibilities curve.*

Remember that if an activity is worth doing, worth doing well, worth doing quickly, it's also worth achieving thoroughly.

Enjoy.

Chapter 1: The Fear of Success

Nobody enters a new area of life without some concern about the outcome of his or her efforts. We can act cautiously or without regard for the consequences, but a cavalier attitude is not generally a part of our makeup. You must have some idea of the potential outcomes possible and a desire to achieve some specific and worthy result for the efforts expended.

Doubt leads to indecision, which leads to inaction, loss of potential returns, and a degree of unhappiness with the result. It may be true that caution is its own reward, but it's also true that without some risk, there will be no return. Otherwise, you will have merely exchanged one set of assets for another.

Uncontrollable Elements

We either have no control or at best exercise only limited control over few happenings. Both death and taxes come to mind.

Many more *happenings* occur over which we have little control. Children leave home and face similar, yet unusual, circumstances as their parents. We get older. We can mitigate the symbols of aging, but we haven't found a way to stop the clock. Accidents happen—people are in the wrong place, at the wrong time, performing the wrong set of tasks. You may—or may not—attribute this to chance, to fate, or to stupidity, but there is no doubt our lives are affected by them.

Tornados, hurricanes, snowstorms, forest fires, and mudslides all affect our lives and while we can take steps to protect us from their effects, there is no doubt but what they alter our lives. Contests, conflicts, wars, poverty, homelessness, illnesses, loss of friends, loss of employment, and other challenges all test our mettle. We exercise little, if any, control over these happenings. Worse, there is often the *illusion* of control where there is no control at all. We find that out to our chagrin.

Situations That Allow Control

There are other situations over which we have some form of control—either of the *happening* itself or of our response to it. Included here is simple decision making. We're frightened of the *what-if's*. Later we'll discuss this fear. Some of us fear public speaking. Novice actors have stage fright. Some elderly people fear computers. Some who feel they are not photogenic might not want to appear on television or in photographs.

Face-to-face meetings paralyze some, and to seek safety, people will often resort to the telephone, and now to text messaging. Many people fear knocking on the door or speaking to a stranger on the street, in a market, or in some non-public location. To minimize our risk, some denigrate their people or their skills in an attempt to avoid loss of face should their efforts fail. Self-deception is an easy pit to fall into.

Fear of loneliness is real to some people, though the cure for that fear is the simplest of all—get with somebody else. Sometimes, fear of being with somebody also is paralyzing. Imagine the fear an older person engenders when returning to school. Some people fear driving any further than ten miles from home and avoid any possible roadway that even appears busy. Some will go miles out of their way to avoid a school or construction zone.

We know that we can learn to handle many situations. We know it. Others have. Why, then, do we fear rejection, vulnerability, success, failure, loss of face, or other things over which we *do* have control? Why then do we erect walls and other defenses to ensure that we are not touched by these fears? We'd rather flee the fear than confront it. Our constant flight from our fears brings on failure. Our constant exposure to failure brings about a self-loathing that, at the very least, defeats the potential for doing anything risky at any time.

Just To See What Happens Next

Perhaps the greatest "happening" we encounter is change. We are beset by change daily. Some changes we experience are improvements. Some are merely annoying. Some may appear disastrous, given our resistance to doing things differently. Change makes its demand on us for one attribute and one alone: flexibility. The degree of flexibility we are willing or able to exhibit determines the adaptability to what's thrown at us by life, by circumstances, and even by the situations into which we insert ourselves.

Nothing can be presented in this or any other book that will cause you to confront your fears and overcome them. All I, or any author, can do is to acquaint you with an important reality—one that you cannot escape: *the seeds of your fears lie in you*—and overcoming them requires your conscious action. Does that mean that fear is never instilled by an overpowering situation or authority? No, of course not, but how realistic is that? Others can help you to identify your fears—but you know what they are. Others can suggest solutions—but you know what must be done.

So the question becomes whether you'll take the steps to deal with the problems and make the moves, slowly at first, to gain the confidence necessary to win those battles, one by one. These are not battles someone else can win for you. I can provide encouragement, but nobody but you, yourself, can give you confidence. You gain confidence merely by doing what you fear. You gain confidence as you gain proficiency.

What we're talking about when we discuss a fear of success is different—we find ways to promote our failure. We have become skilled at making excuses for not doing something; even when it's something we will feel is important to do. Much of what has been written about the subject is psychobabble. Nevertheless, the authors agree on this—*you can handle* any situation you *resolve* to handle. You'd do it in an emergency, and you'd do it naturally. What causes you to fail frequently is that you stop to think about it, and when you do, you talk yourself out of doing what must be done to overcome the fear.

Fear is debilitating if we allow it to be. If dooing the task needs skills we don't have, then the trick is to back away a step and find a way to approach the seemingly impossible. You may well find that it isn't impossible at all. Like some wise man has said, "The difficult we do immediately; the impossible takes a little longer."

When you confront that fear, you have the tools to do so again. If you can prove to yourself that you can handle a situation that has been given to you, what is there to fear? If you have handled the situation once, why is it necessary to fear handling it again? Take time to recognize and reward your problem-solving capabilities.

The problem? You don't trust yourself. You don't trust your ability to assess a problem and resolve it. You don't trust yourself to be able to demonstrate to someone important to yourself that it's not necessary to depend on somebody else. That's not necessary. Let's explore why you resist and what you must do to regain trust.

Removing All Fear

Whatever the situation is, you never will get over it. It never goes away. It will always be there. All that will occur is that your comfort in handling it will increase. The fear diminishes progressively.

How do you increase your trust in yourself? By building confidence by gaining the skill you need and performing it. Prove that you alone must resolve the situation. Do it until your response is automatic; until you no longer have to think it through to do it; until you deny the opportunity to talk yourself out of doing what you fear. Every time you put yourself into a no withdrawal situation, you present yourself with a problem that absolutely needs solution and requires that you provide the solution.

Our fear of success backs into a *perceived* fear of failure. We often see failure as an option merely because we can't visualize success. We often cannot visualize success because we've never taken the time necessary to define just what success is for us.

That becomes the question, doesn't it? If I find I can force myself to stand up before a group and make a presentation, I might get good at it, and somebody will ask me to do it. Heavens! We can't have that. I don't like to get up and talk. However, your second presentation is always better than the first; each will be better than the last. We forget that we were nervous; that somebody might criticize; and that nobody will be interested. What is the outcome? People want to hear us. Groups ask us address meetings. The outcome we feared—success—has come true.

Feel helpless? Resolve to overcome that helplessness. You can do it. Thousands have. You can, too. *Someone else has already felt every fear you have.* Get used to it. You'll not be allowed to invent any new fears.

Everybody Is In the Same Boat

The boat isn't sinking. Look around. Everybody you know is handling an insecurity. Nobody I know was ever born supremely comfortable or outstandingly competent.

I like a quotation from Theodore Roosevelt: "When you're asked if you know how to do something, answer 'yes,' and get busy to find how it's done." You know *something*. And you can do *something*. Get busy doing that something and dig for the information, training, and skills you must yet learn.

Fear is nothing more than a test to prove what you know and can do. It's a test to see if you have the resourcefulness to do something new. It's nothing more than the unknown. It's something that, if you are to be successful, *you must do anyway*. You might just as well get about finding the best way—the right way—to do it. Conquer fear by throwing away the crutch. Perfection is unattainable. Striving for it should be our desire.

Henry David Thoreau said, "Most men live lives of quiet desperation." Quiet desperation will eventually lead to helplessness. Nothing you do will ever be satisfying to you. Nothing. Depression will become your constant companion. The deeper you sink into that the less possible your climbing out of the hole will seem, and therefore will become.

Put Yourself in Charge

The fear will never go away. Never. But you can file it under "insignificant" if you'll get out and do it—and keep doing it until you have demonstrated to everybody—and perhaps even fooled yourself—that the task is a *piece of cake.* Adopt a mantra: "The way to conquer a fear is to do what I fear."

Whatever that task is—do it to the best of your ability and feel the victory when you do it. Resolve not to be defeated. Not all others would wish you success, so do the work that will deliver that success for you.

Conquering fear does something else for you. Think of the times when you have had an adrenaline rush. That's what success brings! An adrenaline rush! A feeling of excitement! The task had to be done. You were the one who could do it. You did it—not perfectly—but you did it. Next time will be better. Next time will be easier. Next time you'll show somebody else how to do it. You'll never learn a task so thoroughly as when you have taught it to somebody else.

Seek the Time and Place to Do It

If you *must* do something, you'll do it. In seconds you'll have passed from "I can't do that" to doing it. If you are asked to stand and share information, you have two things to worry about—what to share and how you'll look. Which is more important? You won't know, so you'll forget them and just do the job. That's what it's about. Just doing the job. You get better when you do the job repeatedly. You'll get better quicker when you seek times and places to do it.

You've heard it since you were a kid. Practice makes perfect. Do you need perfection? Some jobs require it. Handling dynamite is one. For most of what we confront, "close enough" is just fine. You'll know more than your audience. You'll perform better than one who has never done it. Because you can demonstrate what must be done and do it yourself, you have become the expert.

Formalize Your Experience

Think about people whom you consider successful. What makes them different from you? Were they once where you now are? Did they drop from the sky proficient and polished? Or could it be that they wrote a report? Or made a presentation? Or taught a class? Or wrote a press release? Or shared an insight? The fact is that good press increases confidence, which in turn leads to increased competence and often more and better press Perhaps fear isn't the insurmountable obstacle you think it is. Having tasted *any* success, you merely find a way to formalize and capitalize on it.

What would you do if you were successful? Why do you doubt your abilities? Are your goals and objectives merely statements for show and tell? What are your commitment and plans? Are they merely empty wishes? They need determined and decisive action. Action requires that you push yourself front and center and force yourself to do what scares you to the point of terror.

A fear of success may be merely a way to excuse your behavior as you see yourself. You may avoid confronting what you fear, letting the other guy do all the work and get all the glory. The problem with that is you must live with yourself. That is the toughest test of all.

What about that person in the mirror looking back at you? Are there things about him or her that you like or dislike? Can you assess what you see to the exclusion of what you know? Can you fit a picture to that person that may not match the person you know is standing there?

The whole concept of "I think I can, I think I can, I think I can," (story: The Little Engine that Could) is that persistence can often overcome doubt. Sometimes opportunity for persistence doesn't exist. Once you've jumped out of that airplane is not the time to learn the fundamentals of parachuting. But at other times, the very worst that could happen is that you will make a non-fatal mistake. Big deal!

Chapter 2: Fear and Taking Risks

Life, it's said, is a crapshoot. You determine the odds, select your strategy, and take what comes. People who drift with the tide are those who have lives of quiet desperation. People who drift make little forward progress. Theirs is a quiet existence. Among those people are those who would work a minimum wage job that has no responsibility rather than to attempt something that causes them to stretch.

People with ambition don't drift with the tide. They swim upstream against the current. Yes, they assess the odds. They develop a strategy and manipulate the circumstances so the available desirable outcomes are achieved. They take a firm hand in the circumstances surrounding their lives and *make* things happen.

If your life is ever to be better than it is, you'll have to take some risk. You'll have to do something you've never done before. You'll have to "take a chance"—on *something* or *someone*.

What limits you? Or your opportunities? What limits your capabilities or your resources? What limits the outcomes of your efforts? Only *you* limit you. You are the one who holds the keys to your success. Only you. Identify your risks and find a way to overcome them, for it's by doing this that you'll grow.

Immobilizing Fear

How little we understand the taking of risks. Often it happens that we fear a change because it upsets an orderly pattern that has become familiar. Take the situation in which a person who has been paid weekly is suddenly promoted to management and now is paid monthly or semi-monthly. Some people are willing to work for a dependable forty hours rather than to better themselves in a situation that upsets stability. Add to it the financial unpredictability of a commission-only position and you can see the basis for difficult marriages.

If life is to improve—if it is to deliver on the promises of your ambitions—you must take some risks. The unwillingness to take risks paralyzes your willingness to do anything. People want a sure thing. The problem with sure things—they present no challenge. They may provide minimal success, but no growth. To risk is to exceed the limits of the goals you set, and do that requires that you handle some uncertainty.

So much of life is full of the ordinary. So many people are used to the ordinary. To them, the ordinary is *good enough.* If we are to achieve *outstanding* success, then it's the *extraordinary* that must drive us. It's a truth that we make room for what's important to us. It's equally true that those activities demand priority in our lives.

There are successful risk-taking and unsuccessful risk-taking. If you are to take any risk, you must assess what lies before you to chart a course through all the trouble spots you can foresee, that can be detected, that must be handled, and that may be avoided.

Often we may be doing everything right, but it seems that everything is coming out all wrong. We begin to doubt our decisions, get *cold feet,* and withdraw. I like this little quotation:

> **On the plains of hesitation**
> **Lie the bones of those who,**
> **With victory in their grasp,**
> **Paused to rest.**

Withdrawal, because we were not sure, becomes defeat in fact. Hesitancy comes naturally. We've had it drummed into our heads for years: "Haste makes waste."

Taking Risks Is a Learned Exercise

A risk, in purely mathematical terms, involves estimating the potential outcome based on some probability of success. Thus, if in 60 of 100 times of doing something there is a successful outcome, your probability will be 60/100, 60%, or 6 in 10.

The *return* from that success, however, is different with each successful occurrence. If you invested a dollar under one set of circumstances, and the test were successful, then your return might be $1.50. Under another set of circumstances, it might be $2.00. Risk measures the certainty of a positive outcome and estimating the economic return for the investment.

That is the risk of your assets—and in business, that's the way it is. Money invested in business must ultimately produce a positive cash flow return; else you'll not be able to stay in business for long. Emotional risk is something else again. There is an investment in time, in caring, and in interest between two people. More importantly, the situation involves two people who are committed to doing the best for the other.

Outstanding success awaits you—once you seek it. Even the Bible says that you have not because you don't ask. There is much that you don't have because you have not been willing to attempt it. When you have a goal worthy of pursuit, your life has a purpose, and the actions you take in support of those goals fit like the random pieces of a picture puzzle.

How do you learn to take risks? By studying the risks and learning from others who have taken similar risks. By inching forward into the risk, cautiously at first, evaluating the intermediate outcomes. By determining the hazards that may be encountered and either planning to avoid them or seeking to bypass them.

There is a greater concern here—you cannot take a risk if you are unwilling to take a risk. The first step may be to steel your mind to the point that a risk is no *scarier* than breathing. In fact, taking no risk, taking the *safe* route, is the greatest risk of all.

Statistically, you enter the world of risks when you step into your automobile. Does risk keep you from doing it? No. Why? Because you *must* travel from Point A to Point B and there is no alternative. That is what is meant by a situation from which you cannot—or won't—withdraw. Could it be because you have done it so many times you are now used to it? Yes, of course. You have developed competence by repetition. Could it mean that despite the statistics, you are willing to accept the risk? That may be the greatest reason. It had to be done. You know how to do it. The risk is something you have accepted. That's a simple formula to follow. You've done it for years. Risk, then, exists but can be negotiated.

Risk is also something that can be manipulated. Perhaps you drive across town a half-hour earlier to minimize your exposure to rush-hour traffic. Perhaps you drive in the daylight to minimize your exposure to darkness. Perhaps you drive in darkness to minimize the glare of the sun. Perhaps you take a defensive driving course to prepare you for all who have not. Perhaps you invest in a vehicle of substantial size and weight to offer additional protection. On one hand, you have mitigated any potential risk. On the other hand, you have enlisted risk as an ally. It's now all those other, unprepared, people who need to worry.

The No Growth Gamble

Without accepting some risk, there is no growth. *Growth*, as it's used here, means some improvement in our lives—physically, emotionally, or intellectually.

As we grow chronologically, our perspectives change. Beliefs once held fall away as maturity replaces youth. The same is true with risk-taking. With advancing maturity, we are often willing to experiment more, measuring our successes as we proceed. As the number of positive-outcome experiments increases, we are then willing to expand both the investment in the experience and the degree of risk that we are willing to take.

As we grow intellectually, we often find that long-held beliefs fall away. Having been given the opportunity to evaluate what has worked and what has not worked, we select future paths based on what we have learned.

What is your conviction? What makes taking *any* risk worthwhile? There is no one technique for risk taking, and even if there were, technique alone won't satisfy the anxiety you may feel when confronted by a risk. There are things you must consider. Nobody who is satisfied with the way things exist is eligible to take a risk. If no risk is taken, however, no growth is possible. By not taking a risk, you are in fact taking a risk—one over which you have no control.

Can't I Lose If I Take A Gamble?

Just as taking an action with a known risk can produce a return, it can also produce a loss. Things change—and often improve. Given the passage of time and the scarcity of the resource, many gain value. Thus, Louis XIV furniture and 1957 Chevrolets are worth more today than when they were manufactured.

No business risk should be taken where the person taking the risk cannot afford to accept a loss. It makes no sense to go into hock to take a risk where some insight into the potential return is not available. The obverse is just as true. If I'm interested to start a business that has already attracted thousands of people who have operated it successfully, where the first investment is minimal, and where there are sufficient assists to help me to be successful, then it would be wise to try to make it work.

Making It Work Is What It Takes

There is a world of difference between *making it work* and *operating it*—whatever *it* is. Making it work implies that we will do anything in our power to achieve a successful outcome. For everybody unwilling to change, some are not only willing but also impose change on others. Making it work, then, is your opportunity to pull even (at the least) or to pull ahead (at best).

Making it work means investment—of time, finances, and devotion. It's something you must *do.* You can choose to do nothing. If so, you may find that you have believed in false security. Doing what it takes may mean putting up the extra resources to make it happen.

X Steps Ahead; Y Steps Backward

For every risk we take, there is some loss. Sometimes the decision is easy—the two strategies are mutually exclusive. You couldn't do one and simultaneously do the other—for financial, legal, ethical, temporal, or even convenience reasons. Vague fears may be inhibiting, as well. Nothing ventured; nothing gained. Nothing ventured; something lost.

Despite the fears, occasionally you'll paint yourself into a corner where a decision becomes necessary. Nature abhors a vacuum. Now the risk has been taken for you and you face the outcome.

Risks are intensely personal. We are often willing to take *repetitive* risks where there is a demonstrable lack of potential, rather than to take the few risks where it's known that there *is* a return. Example: the lottery. You may have to play to win, but the odds are long, indeed.

There are risks of hazard. Why does anybody do something where the risk is so inherently obvious? The reasons will vary. People will do things because they *can* and because the financial, emotional, physical, or promotional reward is sufficient to justify. Alternately, they can afford any loss. For most of us, risks of hazard need not exist.

The Timing of Risk

Should you take a risk now? Today? That depends. In the simplest of terms, if the potential gains outweigh the potential costs, the risk should be assessed. It would also be useful to review your history. What risks have you taken in the past and what have been the outcomes from those risks?

Pretend To Care

Successful risking often involves some bravado. Once you have gathered and evaluated all the data available, you must raise your courage and go out on a limb. You must put yourself on the line. You must at least pretend to care.

Ultimately, if you are to be successful, you must care *very* much. The reason for pretending to care is that it allows you to avoid making excuses for inaction. Once you have begun to tell yourself that you do care about the outcome, there will be an active belief—and active belief is the first step in perseverance.

It's difficult to take any risk or derive any productive output if you aren't convinced you are interested in the work and the outcome. Satisfaction can be derived from setting a goal and taking the steps to make it. Monday morning quarterbacks abound. It's up to us to determine what must be done, how much should be done, and the actions that must be performed.

Chapter 3: Going Out On a Limb

"'Impossible' is a word found only in the dictionary of fools," said Napoleon. "Nothing's impossible, I have found," goes an old show tune. When you adopt that attitude, you have no choice but to be successful.

When making decisions about the future there is nobody less objective than we. It's not that we cannot evaluate our risks objectively. We can. It's not that we can't see what's involved. We can. We often become so wrapped up in the novelty and excitement of a new idea that we fail to stop and evaluate what lies before us. It's more fun and exciting to push ahead, often without the facts before us.

The Necessity of the Risk

What makes this opportunity worth pursuing now? Often things change sufficiently to justify taking the risk. Does this answer a need or merely satisfy a desire? How often do we make foolish mistakes simply because we wish to do so?

Does pursuit of this opportunity support the goals you set? Is the potential gain greater than the potential loss? Remember that embarking on any activity often will require some short term loss while you establish yourself. Have you gained sufficient knowledge to make the risk? Have you tested the demand for pursuit of the risk? Are you unique—will there be competition? You'd better hope there is. It lends credibility.

If you take this risk, what other opportunity must you forgo? If you fail to take the opportunity, will someone else? Can you accomplish the opportunity another way? Often, while not directly competitive, there are complementary opportunities.

The Timing of the Risk

What about this opportunity forces a decision now? Is this a good time to act? If so, why? If not, why not? If delayed, will the opportunity evaporate? If it does, what? How does the timing fit with your resources? It's natural to wonder if you dare risk your resources, so it comes down to ambition: are you willing to *make* your franchise or your opportunity work?

What forces your hand? What is the impetus? You

have the money and the ambition, but the cost is about to rise? You don't have the money but you are willing to risk some sum for the future? There is the possibility of some territorial exclusivity? If it must be done now or somebody else will get it, then you must be able to provide its payoff before making the move.

What will be lost if you don't take the risk now? Will there ever be a better time? How do you know? Lethargy is your greatest enemy. If the time is golden, and all the other factors fall into line—and, of course, if you have the resources—then, by all means, make a move.

Support for the Action

Who wishes you to succeed, and why? Who's in your corner? A spouse? A parent? Are they willing to put their time and resources into risk to assist you? Does anyone or anything pressure you to make the move? Why? Who wishes you to fail, and why? Why would anyone wish you to fail? Certainly the competition will. Is there a motive for success because of these people? Spite is a great motivator. Just simply telling somebody that he or she can't or shouldn't succeed is a phenomenal motivator.

Have you financial or emotional supports? It takes money to start a business. Can you get a loan? Do you have sufficient credit? What will it cost for others' participation in your action? Grants and loans are good.

Sweat equity—exchanging work for money—will help.

Is this a joint effort? Will you take on a partner? What are the rights and privileges of the partnership? If you decide to remove yourself, will your partner gain your share? Does a potential associate share your vision? When you attract a partner, look for one who wants from your project the same things you want. If not, what then will you do when commitment flags?

When others look at you

How much success is enough? If you're instantly successful, how will you grow? Growth is a worthwhile objective, but slow growth is preferred. Instant growth allows one to become quickly overextended.

Would someone else's discouragement kill your ambition? We meet many people who are simply naysayers. They envy your willingness to take a risk, but they wouldn't dare do it themselves.

Would you act when discouraged? Would you take decisive action to pull yourself up? Success takes positive and proactive movement..

Do you worry about others' concerns about your actions? If what you're doing is legitimate and you have thought it through, don't bother to care whatever anybody thinks.

If you are successful, what then? What's next? How will you build on your success? If a dream is the wish your heard makes, then it's time to get dreaming again. Don't let *anybody* say that you can't.

How much challenge is enough? Challenge is the oil that greases the joints, and age makes no difference.

What About You, Yourself?

Have you "talked yourself into" taking a given action? How realistic has been your evaluation? How often do you believe yourself? Do you have a record of accomplishment? Keep good records. Repeat your successes and build on them. Conditions? Study them as quickly and thoroughly as you can, and make a decision.

Can you itemize your fears? What scares you? Can you answer or counteract every fear? If you don't take this risk, what will you do instead? If not, and you don't take this option, you will have to wait until the next one comes along. The problem then is that your motivation will decrease. Better to make a correctible mistake than to avoid making a decision.

If you don't see it through, will you have a sense of loss? "I think I can, I think I can" is one thing. "I wish I had" is something else again. Failure exacts a heavy emotional toll. Voluntary failure—giving up without a try—is the worst of all. We live with too many "if onlys."

Are you prepared to take this risk? Financially? Emotionally? What knowledge will you need? Can you get it quickly? Get the knowledge. You'll be shaky about it at first, but act as if you know—and what you don't know, you'll learn quickly.

Can You Forecast the Points of Difficulty?

If so, have you contingency plans? Anticipation is important. Lead-time provides positive preparation when it's needed. Again, don't go into any endeavor figuring that everything will go well. Is there any situation that would arrest your success? Changes in policy and regulation that can be seen will require some planning.

Planning for Life After the Decision

How will you evaluate the success of your decisions? It's possible to make bad decisions that work out well. Think, for a minute, what the motivation is behind any fad. Remember the pet rock? As my father said at the time, "What ninny decided that people would buy a rock in a box and name it?" Many, however, did just that.

How will you determine whether the help you got was suitable? Can you change focus during the trip to your goal? What would be the *sunk cost* should you decide to abort? How much can you afford to lose before it seriously affects your net worth? Once you know this, you can place a value on failure, but don't dwell on it. It's an alert mechanism only. Get out and make it happen.

How will it affect you should you decide to abort? If you're in a hole and are having trouble getting out, stop digging. What about the relations you have built? Customers and employees are people and each of them is fighting their own demons daily. Don't burn any bridges.

Will you know *when* you have become successful? If you've set a goal to which you must stretch, and you met or exceeded it, you can legitimately celebrate. Will you have a plan of attack for the next growth spurt? Set a new goal that requires a stretch of yourself and your resources, and get about it.

Will completion of this risk create any further risks? If a Chevrolet is what you have driven every day of the last two years, don't allow a good year to lull you into upgrading to a Lexus. Put yourself in a higher bracket before you're ready to do so, and you invite trouble.

Can those risks be foreseen during this time? If they can, you can take steps to reduce their effects. Can you formalize the risk-taking process; remove the pressure? Spend a little to keep a lot more. Take the sage advice and bootstrap it into further growth.

Taking Responsibility for Your Risks

The reluctance of people to take risks can often be traced to childhood, when strong parental influences protect a child from overt dangers. Accepting responsibility for your risks is imperative. Risks imposed are often not avoidable and therefore demand handling. Elective risks may be avoided, but we know what that means—no growth, no improvement in standard of living, and no personal satisfaction of accomplishment. Success is a *happening* waiting for your support.

If you don't take charge of your dream, who will do it for you? If somebody else does anything to contribute to your success, what will be your sense of accomplishment? What have you shouted to the world? Have you not announced that you are incapable of taking charge of your life and directing your actions towards a rewarding goal? Nobody will take the risk for you and stand by to see you receive the rewards. Refuse to take the risks and you deny yourself the successes of your life. It's not a comfortable way to live.

Because there's risk, it's possible the risk won't pay. You are now in jeopardy. If you don't do something, and soon, you stand to lose whatever you have invested in the risk. You must now marshal resources to see that the risk *does* pay. Only you can make it happen. Only you.

Passion Sparks Your Fuse

Once you have taken responsibility for your risks, you must do many things to make it happen. Whip your passion into frenzy, because it's your faith in yourself that will make *your* dream come true. Passion sparks the fuse that begins the chain reaction to that series of explosions known as success.

Causing the Juices to Flow

There is nothing you can hear, nothing you can read, nothing that someone else can do, nothing that you can dream about that will place in your gut the passion to pursue your dream. Nor can any of that cause you to pursue your activity until it consumes you. Does that mean you either have it or you don't? *Not on your life!* You can develop that fire in the belly to do what needs to be done if you'll adopt a few perspectives.

Try this one: *excellence is not optional.* How does one become excellent? What is excellence? It starts with knowledge. It continues with presentation. It finishes with satisfaction. If you *expect* excellence from yourself and from others you'll provide it. This means you must be serious about your endeavor.

Here's another: *excellence knows no time clock.* How many hours per week are you willing to give to your dream? If your dream is merely a hobby, it may be few. If you perceive your dream to be a platform to something greater, your perspective will change. You have a choice between developing good habits or bad habits. Excellence can be a habit. Demand more of yourself and you'll receive more from yourself.

Excellence mandates that you "walk a mile" in another's shoes, that you gain empathy and understanding, and that you deliver on the promise that you make to yourself and to others.

Of course, *excellence requires commitment.*

Making Your Dream Important to You

If you develop a sense of urgency about your work and pay attention to details, you'll find that your passion for your work will increase. It's possible to develop passion while diminishing stress. Only in a life-or-death struggle must they be related. Could it be planning to make ten calls and forcing yourself to make the eleventh? Could it be making a plan, then working your plan? Here's something to remember: *proper planning prevents poor performance.* You may ask, "How can I plan? If your field is sales, plan by knowing what this customer buys and when those items are offered as a special sale.

Your focus is business. Have you an adequate supply

of business cards? Is your promotional literature prepared? Have you a box of it with you? Samples? Supplies? Are you ready to do business? Do you believe in yourself, your company, and your products? Negative attitudes can kill the spark and remove the passion.

Do you look at life through the windshield or through the rear view mirror? It doesn't matter what lies behind-- just what lies ahead.

We get anxious when something goes afoul of the process and others express discontent. It's no different anywhere else. The same human imperfections that plague you now will plague you there. The best you can do is to promise the best you can do. Then rejoice! It's nothing that you and God together can't handle.

All You Must Do Is Find It

A passion for something lies in you, and only you can tap the well. It's important, if you are to be successful, that you build a fire under your butt develop a comprehensive plan to improve your performance. Remember, each day you get better or you get worse. It's your choice. The building of that incentive means that you must push yourself. Only you can motivate you. Not until you make a firm decision that you'll try something and see it through, no matter what, will you develop that fire.

Who(m) Do You Trust?

Is yours a *will* or a *won't*? Have you ever failed—at anything? Everyone fails at something, sometimes. Does failure bring discouragement or determination? If it brings discouragement , changing that to determination is an act of your conscious will—and if you can do that, there will be no *won't*. Evangelist Billy Sunday said, "Fear knocked at the door and faith answered; and there was no one there." Have faith that your capabilities, married to your commitment, will see you through to success.

Chapter 4: Ambivalence to Ambition to Action

He was called the Sultan of Swat for a reason. He hit more home runs than anyone else of his era. George Herman (Babe) Ruth set the record for annual home runs—60—in 1927, a number that would not be passed until Roger Maris did it with 61 in 1961. The record is now 73 home runs in a single season.

By the time he hung up his spikes in 1937, Ruth had hit 714 home runs, a figure that stood until Hank Aaron surpassed it with 755 in the early 1970s. Ruth was a giant of his times and is remembered for his successes. What is barely remembered is the number of times he struck out. Until surpassed by Reggie Jackson, Ruth had struck out more times (1,330) than anyone in the history of baseball.

History is replete with people who failed and overcame failure. Failure is not the number of times you fall—it occurs only if you never pick yourself up again and keep trying. To be successful, along the way you must select a direction, crank up your resolve, persevere in the execution of a plan, and see the process through.

En Garde! Charge!

If you allow yourself to think that failure is possible, then failure will be a probability, and often a certainty. I cannot allow you be so ambivalent to think that the outcome of the trial that confronts you is an either/or situation, where the *either* is success and the *or* is failure.

Win/Lose vs. Win/Win

Merely because a situation has a sixty percent probability of success does not mean that there is a forty percent probability of failure. No, that forty percent is merely the probability of something *less* than success, assuming you experience something less than the degree of return you hope to achieve. Every action you take is a trial—an experiment—in some degree of success. It may be a small. It may be large. It's still a success. Whether you see it as a success is a function of your perspectives.

Ambition Requires That You Try Again

If you perceive that forty percent to be your risk of failure, then you have given extraordinary odds to the potential of lack of an extreme success. The either/or nature of this perspective anticipates failure. In a win/lose model, the selected strategy is either successful or unsuccessful, and there is no middle ground. If you are successful, you'll receive the rewards for your efforts. If you are not successful, you'll receive nothing besides your self-scorn for not being the best possible.

The win/win model of your dream recognizes that despite your best intentions and efforts, it sometimes happens that your efforts are less than successful. Note that the words used are *less than successful*—not *failure*.

You must conclude that *all* results from your dream trial are successful, some more than others. If you can perceive that by giving it all you can possibly give, you'll achieve positive outcomes, then the choice of direction you take, once you make the move, is what will determine your success.

To make that decision you must do some investigation about what might work most successfully, but your success comes in the confidence that whichever you select, in reason, there will be some positive return from your efforts.

Success Is Assurable

Give up the notion that you either succeed or fail. You'll always succeed. As you gather the knowledge, support, and experience necessary to achieve the success you wish, draw on the confidence that you can do it and nobody can do it as well as you can do it.

Characteristics of Ambition

Aspiration is worth having, but aspiration without action is hollow. Drive—the intense pursuit of the aspiration—is what sets the timetable for the accomplishment of the aspiration. Are there degrees of intensity? Yes. At the lowest intensity, the interest is high, the timetable is extended, and people may well be driven, but to distraction. It's at the highest intensity where drive becomes an obsession.

The Killer Instinct

The second part of ambition is making the most of your opportunities. I call that the *killer instinct*. I'm not convinced that one can instill the killer instinct in another, but I am convinced that one can train oneself for it. It does take a conscious evaluation of every opportunity that presents itself.

To do that, one must invest energy, approach the opportunity aggressively, employ some capital, and put forth the effort. Refusing to try your best, for whatever reason, will signal your unwillingness to be as successful as you can be. Just as is necessary in playing a good game of golf or tennis, you must keep your eye on the ball.

Developing Your Confidence

Next must come confidence. If you have none of that, drive and instinct will be of no avail. Confidence comes with experience and success, and nobody is born with that. It must be developed. It's insufficient merely to work hard and hope for the best outcome. If you are to be successful, use some bravado—put yourself out front and vow to attain some form of success that will, in turn, provide both experience and confidence.

Take a risk of esteem. Don't be afraid that you don't know the answer. Tell someone you don't know the answer. Chances are they do. In fact, try telling someone you don't know the answer, even if you do. You'll be amazed how much you learn. You'll be surprised how impressed someone else is when either he gets to share what he knows or together you discover the answer.

Exert Control

Ambition means that you exert control where you can. There are many things you can control—costs, opportunity, choices, selection of options, and degrees of reward. You can be powerful, not powerless over your environment.

It's your choice to function above capacity; even above the capacities that you even *think* you are capable.

Often that control requires you to confront the question: With whom are you in competition? If you are ambitious, the answer must always be with yourself.

What makes you successful is not your competition with someone else. It's always your competition with yourself—the best you can do today, which must be better than what you did yesterday.

It's your hope of becoming something better than you are that make all the difference. "Would you like to swing on a star? Carry moonbeams home in a jar? Or be better off than you are…" goes the refrain on an old Bing Crosby tune. If, indeed, a dream is a wish your heart makes, then don't forget the old dreams. Work them over in your mind and your heart. Build the fire under them. Get the fuel onto them. Daily ask yourself, "Why not?" Learn who you are. Perhaps you are born to rebel—to do things differently from what has ever been done.

Ambition Is As Ambition Does

Take a positive step each day to save yourself from the ordinary. Start paying attention to your inner voice. Create your identity. Learn positive things about yourself. Those are available, you know. Your life is in your hands. Your ambition is the way out of a trap that you may not have created for yourself, but that you can escape through your efforts.

Select a no lose model to follow. Pick a strategy and test it. Don't talk yourself out of it. You'll be successful despite the outcome. That fearless self—the person inside you—needs always to ask "Am I good at what I want to be good at?" If you are, then you cheat yourself and people around you if you do otherwise. Happiness about your life is far more important than mere payment.

Standing on your own two feet becomes a habit with exercise. If you want something bad enough, there is always a way to get it. All you need to do is to rid yourself of no win thinking. Anything is possible—if you'll merely take the choice of two yeses. Every time you encounter something that forces you to *handle it* you strengthen your resolve. There is no need to get anyone's approval. Throw away the picture you had. Substitute a brand new picture of your becoming successful.

And that picture of yourself becomes a challenge. So what if problems ensue? You'll handle it. So what if … if … if… It doesn't matter. You'll handle it. You're up to the challenge. You can do it. "Nice work if you can do it, and you can do it if you try."

Take Action Now

Thinking about doing it will never be sufficient. Here are some action steps that will get you moving:

Strike the notion of failure. You'll never be a failure because you didn't make it—only if you never try. You can *earn* failure every bit as well as you can earn success. The latter is preferable.

Define a winning strategy. It feels better not to lose. Recognize that there are degrees of winning. Keep ahead of the expenses and you'll succeed. If your expenses continually run ahead of your income, then one of two things has occurred—you have underestimated the potential or there is something different you must do. Only in making a positive change will you find that elusive success. Getting by is not enough. You have to want to survive. You have to want to excel. You must be driven, not to distraction, but to excellence.

Document not only your determination but also the steps you'll take to stoke that determination. Plan not only for the activity, but also for handling yourself. Take paper and write: "when _____ happens, I'll do: _____."

Gain the support of positive people. Read everything motivating you can find. Listen to every motivational tape you can find. Examine what others have done and learn from it. Take your pick of the experiences of others. Evaluate everything and everybody. Study. Study.

Understudy someone who is doing what you wish to do. Offer to work free for a while and be a sponge—soak up everything you can. Document it. Research what you don't yet know about. Watch. Document. Try. Experience. Do it!

Locate your financial support. What must you have to begin? Don't wait until you have everything you need—either you'll never have it or its price will escalate so significantly that you'll not be able to afford it then. Plan to obtain additional support in its necessary time.

Negotiate the best terms you can find, put down the first payment, and sign the lease. Or buy the inventory. Or place the advertising. No time like now. You are on the line. Not your husband. Not your wife. Not your parents. You. You must make this work.

Schedule your activities to permit you to actively begin. Build what needs to be built before you need to install them. Buy what you need before you need it so waiting won't be a problem. If a move is involved, plan the move, to the last detail. If a set-up is involved, plan the setup, even if you must construct a model or draw a picture. Do you need tables? Do you need baskets and frou-frou? Need to take pictures? Do it!

If others are to be involved, learn about them—their desires, assets, liabilities, and contributions. Prepare them as you have prepared yourself. Instill the passion that you feel for your dream, remembering that you are enlisting them to make your dream come true—not theirs. If you can help them locate and develop their dreams, so much the better.

Finally, make no plans to make no mistakes. That will never work. You'll make mistakes and you'll learn from them. You'll take what you learn, consolidate your position, and strike out again. If you fall, that's OK. Just pick yourself up, dust yourself off, and start all over again.

Now go get 'em, Tiger! Outstanding success awaits you!

Chapter 5: Preparing the Action Plan

Is A Good Attitude All You Need?

If attitude isn't everything, it's way ahead of whatever's in second place. A positive attitude isn't all you need, of course—but it's the most important part of your success in business or a relationship. It, and it alone, can make or break any endeavor.

A positive attitude is not always natural. It's a decision, repeated so often that it becomes a part of the fabric of your life. You must seek positive things, positive people, and positive experiences. You must view edifying movies, listen to uplifting music, and expand the scope of your acquaintances to those who will have a positive influence on your life. It follows that you should avoid those who don't. Attitude is fragile, needing constant attention and the re-enforcement of like-minded people.

Look in the yellow pages and you'll be unable to

locate a meeting of the Positive Attitude Society. That's odd. You'd think there would be a great interest in finding ways to increase one's positive attitude, if it's that important. Think about that for a moment. Where do the positive people gather? Is it at discotheques, dance clubs, rock concerts, or bars? Or might it be at churches, boys and girls clubs, volunteer activities, or sports teams? Further, can we distinguish a type of activity that begets positive attitudes? Do you suppose it's in self-oriented activities or in activities that are other-oriented?

However you have answered those questions, allow me to provide a singular answer—you'll find the most positive people where someone is doing something for someone else. Big Brothers/Big Sisters is one such group. Homeless shelters are others. Services for people—where you give not only your money, but also your time. There are many people, down on their luck, who need your outstanding attitude and positive contributions to their lives today. By far the most interesting part of a volunteer activity is that the pay is extraordinary.

In any endeavor, you can decide that what you are about to do can be tedious and boring. Or you can decide it will be thrilling, enlightening, joyous, and beneficial. Be aware that a decision about one or the other must be made and you must be the one to make it.

It's natural to *get down* once in a while. It happens to all. Modern language calls it a *funk*. Funks aren't much fun, and you'll not begin to enjoy yourself or what you are trying to do unless you break it and get back into the sunshine of a positive perspective on your life and endeavors. It takes some work on your part. Nobody can do it for you.

It's easy to assume that our attitudes are acceptable, and if to us, they must be to others. That's often not true, but we do like to delude ourselves. To others around us, our attitudes may not be acceptable—merely tolerated.

We need an *outstanding* attitude. It's the attitude that permits you to bounce out of bed in the morning with a smile on your face, a melody in your heart, and a determination to tackle life today. Perhaps there are so few of us who can do that consistently, morning after morning. But that doesn't mean we can't work on it! We are creatures of emotion. We react to the *ups* in life. We react to the *downs,* as well. What brings us outstanding emotions are often the *mountaintop* experiences that leave us convinced that we are in full control of our lives, our opportunities, and their outcomes.

What brings us down is myriad—the bills, the job, the pressures of family, the status of our health, just to name a few. Finding balance in one's life, then, requires a conscious effort on our parts. The trick is to try to change as many *down* emotions into *up* emotions as possible—and if not possible, at least into neutral emotion that neither builds us up nor bogs us down.

Read about positive attitudes, and you'll find that few people, if any, are naturally positive. They must work at it. They must stop, take stock, and determine that today *will* be not just OK, but *outstanding*! It would perhaps be useful for someone to develop a PAA—a Positive Attitudes Anonymous organization where we can all stand up, say, "Hi, I'm (insert your name), and I'm normally a 'down' person—but just for today, I'll *have* a positive attitude." We'll work on tomorrow, tomorrow. Yesterday was good. Join with me now in one verse of Just Let A Smile Be Your Umbrella.

There arc ways to build a positive attitude. Some are presented here. There are many seminars to attend, CDs to listen to, and books to read, that will help you begin each morning with at least the knowledge that you, too, can bring off that positive attitude you'll need to do your activities today. Like the smile that can be passed around, it can happen with your outstanding attitude, as well.

It May Be a Matter of Perspective

Often how we see our lives is a function of our perspectives. The best illustration I know of this is the response from two carpenters working on a house. When asked what he was doing, the first responded that he was building a house, as anyone could see. The second responded that he was helping build a great city. That positive attitude, applied to the ultimate purpose, colors everything we do, and become an important determinant of success or failure.

When asked how I am, I often respond with: "I'm wonderful—I'm so wonderful that were I to become more wonderful, I'd have to be twins! And the world isn't ready for that!" That, to me, is far better than merely saying that I'm fine, or that I'm OK. It's better than talking about my pains and aches.

I begin that conversation with the assumption the person who asked the question wanted to know the answer and because of my response, he or she can move from that point in a positive direction; and with my help, for a great distance in that direction. I further assume that I can influence someone else's attitude; that my positive attitude can rub off onto the other person. Perhaps you have heard it said—if you see someone without a smile, give him yours.

For me, having had a brush with death, every day *is* wonderful. I can remember a time when I would respond with an attitude of humdrum.

Let Thankfulness Control Your Day

Today has been beautiful. I've lived and loved another day. My needs are met. There is enough of a surplus to share with another. For some, it's "though I walk through the valley of the shadow of death, I shall fear no evil." For others, it's "I have peace of mind and freedom from all fear." What strikes me about these is that the way to overcome fear is to begin the day with gratitude. Then, as the song says, "spread joy up to the maximum, bring gloom down to the minimum, latch onto the alternative; don't mess with Mr. In-Between."

Napoleon Hill, in his book, *The Master Key To Riches*, called this his "Princes of material prosperity, of sound physical health, of peace of mind, of hope, of faith, or love, of romance, and of overall wisdom." He held that if you have these attributes, you have the enduring assets of (get this): "past failures, defeats, errors of judgment and of deed, all fears, mistakes, disappointments, and adversities of every nature." That's powerful stuff. Because of all this, you can "take control of your mind, the one thing over which you have complete control." He had a daily conference with each of his "Princes."

Wait a minute! These *assets* are all negative. Consider that each of those becomes the launching pad for changing your past and present into a very valuable future. It's been said that the past is gone, the future hasn't happened, and that today is our gift—that's why it's called the *present*. If you change your thinking, you'll change your life—and the change in your thinking will be a natural outgrowth of your change of attitude. Positive change will produce a corresponding outcome.

Think about the embarrassments of your life—things you wish had never happened. Why do you think about them now, later in life? Why can't you put them out of your mind? Because each taught a lesson, often a lesson you took to heart, and you revisit them to repeat and strengthen the learning. It's what my Mom used to call "the little man" inside my head, my conscience. It's my subconscious mind in most of the others, and the subconscious mind can be trained in positive ways. Every time something goes wrong and adversity overtakes us, the subconscious begins to search for the opportunity it's made available.

At the Beginning of a Perfect Day

When you begin any new endeavor, take some time to define goals. Defining them doesn't do any good if their definition is, in fact, indefinite. All generalities are admirable. Why do we wish that? Do you want the award or the reward? They may not be the same.

Effort brings forth the reward that brings forth the

benefit. The service you render will attract the money you control. The money you control establishes the growth in those services and provides resources for developing the intangibles of your life. The growth is what brings an overwhelming obstacle into clear focus and achievement. Recognize that the growth and its accompanying reward release you from obligations that are just as overwhelming.

Positive Attitudes Overcome Lack of Purpose

By any definition of success, the purpose of that outstanding positive attitude is to achieve the best. *Best* is easily defined. It surpasses anything that is seen in the activity. It's better performance that anyone has ever done. It's satisfaction to the point that nobody need question motive or results. It's extraordinary. It goes against the ordinary that the world demands we accept.

If your attitude leads you to develop a goal to be the best at whatever you do, that provides a definite and measurable purpose. The building of a positive attitude requires that you establish a purpose, develop a strategy—perhaps to even make the sacrifices to empower that strategy, and take the steps necessary to make it happen. That purpose will be achieved if you continually remind yourself of it. A positive attitude, then, becomes self-nagging about the grandiosity of your plans and the achievement of the intermediate steps. Left unattended it becomes a haunting self-nagging.

Motivation Can Be Its Own Incentive

In the early part of the 20th Century, Andrew Carnegie made his millions in steel mills. His firm became what you now know as United States Steel. Carnegie was a pragmatic man. One day, while moving through one of his Pittsburgh mills, he came upon a man who was slowly loading a hopper car with coal. He watched the man work. He had the power to fire the man for not hustling. Instead, Carnegie asked the man if he would like to make more money. The worker acknowledged interest.

Carnegie told the man he would do two things for him. First, he would supply a larger shovel. Second, he would pay the man his current wage for his current average number of completed hopper cars—but for every extra car the man loaded during his shift, he would be paid more. Thus was born what we call the incentive system in this country. Note that the improvement in the man's circumstances followed, and was the direct result of, a change and improvement in a tool. What do you suppose that says about gaining knowledge, tapping the knowledge and experiences of other successful people, and devouring everything you can get your hands on?

Carnegie didn't apply his positive motivation only to the labor force. He extended it to his office staff, as well. You know the name Charles Schwab. The original, Charles M. Schwab, became Carnegie's Chief Financial Officer and ultimately the head of United States Steel. For office people, including Mr. Schwab, Carnegie began a measurement that became known as *going the extra mile.* Those who were promoted to positions of increasing responsibility were people who offered exceptional service and gained extraordinary knowledge. They were not merely the ones who worked longer hours. They were those who added value to themselves and, in turn, added value to Carnegie's operation. His message to Schwab and others was: "If you have your heart fixed on what you want there is nothing I can do to stop you from getting it." Carnegie, by the way, concentrated his later years on philanthropy, especially in libraries and higher education. He gave everything away.

The message for us, then, is that people who move with a definite purpose will find that they overtake everyone on the ladder and will usually surpass the goal that they set for themselves. It should come as no surprise, then, that failure begins with people having little or no purpose, with life in general or their activities in particular. They are adrift on a sea made restless by those who would stir the water, until either they float to the wayside (note that I wouldn't say "sink") or somebody reaches them with the message.

Find Success with a Definite Purpose

Those of you with a definite purpose have taken a most valuable step towards developing that positive attitude that leads to success. If you don't yet have that definite purpose, take some time to write it. Repeat it to yourself day by day. Write it out and post it on the door, refrigerator, mirror, door, and wherever you'll cast your eyes. Every time you see it, say the words—aloud if you can, for the mind's ear is a powerful entrée to the subconscious—but softly to yourself if necessary. Then devour every avenue of learning the how, where, what, why, and when necessary to take you to the goal you set and encourage you to stretch to the goal you'd like to reach. With your positive attitude, it's *very* possible.

One of the benefits of having a definite purpose is that you bypass deliberation. You won't have to question endlessly every decision. You'll make the decision. If it can be improved, you'll improve it. Gather all the facts, evaluate them, and decide. Now. Immediately. Don't study it to death. Don't wait until you feel success is assured. You'll discover that if you have this definiteness of purpose, it will extend to other parts of your life, as well. For those who recruit, please consider that if your prospect waffles, she'll always waffle, for she has no distinct and definite purpose. You can't give it to her. You'd better find one who does.

And the Lesson Is ...

Let's carry four lessons away from this discussion:

- Embrace every opportunity by defining a definite purpose and committing to it. Consider the two shoe salesmen who, on arriving at a remote African village, wired their impressions back to the home office. The first said he was returning to the office because "nobody here wears shoes." The second placed a large order and exclaimed: "Nobody here has any shoes!" I like an old hymn here: "If your heart beats right, if your heart beats right, there's a song of gladness in the darkest night; every cloud will be a rainbow, if your heart beats right." The positive attitude turns the glooms into joys.

- Prepare yourself to go the extra mile to make it happen. Plan that extra service and go out of your way to give it. Don't make it accidental. Make it your task to extend yourself to someone in need of what you have to offer. Introduce the wonder of your knowledge and your devotion to others. If you take those extra steps, you can't help but be rewarded. There will be times that it won't help. That's OK. You can't please some people some of the time. Most of the time it will. It's the maintenance program for the positive attitude. It feeds on itself in ever-widening circles, the antithesis of a pity party.

- Be willing to celebrate and to share your success. Others need what you have to offer. Others need to know that you'll support them, as well.

- Find a motivational tape or CD and play it. Read a motivational book. Learn a lesson or two from these people—you'll be amazed how it will improve both your life and your activities.

Then the concern for attitude will become moot. Your attitude and motivation will guide you to make the plans, take the steps, perform the plan, and reap the rewards.

When You Come to the End of a Perfect Day...

Whom do you thank? How do you express gratitude? Are others aware that you have given thanks? You might think about that.

Retrospect is important, as well. You licked today; you met the problems and provided the solutions. What about tomorrow? What is the plan? What problems can you foresee and how are you prepared to meet them? What exercise of your risk-taking is scheduled for your operations. It is always good to document the plan and how the risk was handled, as a guide for future operations.

Chapter 6: Greasing the Wheels

How do you define ambition? Just what does ambition mean? How can you tell if you have ambition? How will you approach your ambitions? How will you know you have realized your ambition? These and other questions are the focus of this chapter.

"What would you like to be when you grow up, little boy?"

"I wanna be a fireman!"

"And why do you want to be a fireman?"

"They drive red trucks and spray water on fires and stuff."

You can no doubt remember the dialog or something similar, as some curious adult asked you about what you wished to do with your life. How old were you? Maybe three? The answers might have been football players, nurses, doctors, airplane pilots, secretaries, "the boss," rock musician, or whatever happened to catch your interest at that point in your life. As you grew older and your exposure to the world grew, so, too, did your aspirations and ambitions for the realizations of a life's work take shape?

For me, it was to be a teacher. I can't tell you why. As a youngster, I played school. As a middle-schooler I joined the organization for future teachers. As a high schooler I joined the debating society, the band, the orchestra, and the glee club. I wrote for the school paper. I sought things structured and intellectual. Guidance tests, especially a test called Strong's Vocational Interest Blank, indicated that I should go into teaching, and pointed out that I would never be able to do anything with my hands.

Next came teacher's college—in the days when there were such. As quickly as I got in, I got out. Just didn't fit. Something was not right (besides late teen hormones). I had little interest in teaching elementary children. Thus was created a paradox and a predicament that would take years to resolve.

Turnover Requires Focus

In 1956, I dropped out of college and joined the USAF. For more than six years I did clerical and other structured tasks assigned to a military grunt. I merely existed. No ambition. No drive. No goals. No focus. One day in 1962, at Ft. Meyer, VA, I was assigned to a Master Sergeant whom I quickly came to detest, and with so large a disdain, I began to explore my opportunities. There were few. I had a focus—to escape my Master Sergeant, who happened to be the base supply NCO (non-commissioned officer). Anyone with military experience can testify to the fact that the supply NCO is *the* politician on any military base. I learned then that nothing political would ever be a part of my future.

And Bravado

One day I was performing temporary duty at the headquarters office when I encountered something I seldom saw—a bulletin, the organization's two-page daily newspaper. It was advertising for people to take an aptitude examination for computer programming. I had no idea about what a computer was, much less any knowledge about programming it. Here, however, was the possibility of an escape from Sergeant Politico. He forbade me to take the exam, but I learned that I had a right to do so, so I applied for it, filled out the paperwork, and sent it off to Headquarters Command, Bolling Field.

I was taking my child to the doctor on the morning the examination was scheduled. I had been directed to appear to the test, but the NCO had conveniently "forgotten" that, despite a four-day notice. I learned about it from someone else in the office that afternoon, when I returned to work, and after the test had been conducted. Sergeant Politico had received a call the previous week directing me to appear at 11 a.m. to take the test. Because he had originally forbidden me, he purposely chose not to tell me. I could have been jailed that afternoon, because he got an earful. I left the office and went straight to the Chaplain, a much more powerful politician. I was tested the following morning in a special session. It was tense in that office for a few days.

Life Is a Game of Inches

Thirteen people sat for that examination. Out of 100 points, the top scorer rated a 98%. I rated a 95%. The third member rated 92%. *Two people were selected!* Life is a game of inches. Two days later, I was transferred to Headquarters Command and in a week, I was in school to learn how to program the Univac File Computer.

Airman Topscorer didn't take to it, but did take to computer operations, which he did for a year before getting out of the USAF. For me, it was a resurrection. I was back using my cranium. A thirst for knowledge had been reborn in me, along with a passion to soak up all I could in the shortest possible time.

I helped build the USAF's first computerized personnel system, and by 1964, that project was complete and the Air Force was looking for another assignment for me. One day I was called into the commander's office and was told: "Congratulations, you're now a teacher." I'd come full circle. I was to join the staff of the Air Force's Data Processing Technical School in northern Texas.

Sometimes Not What It Seems

After arrival Sheppard AFB, I was advised that a bureaucratic snafu had occurred and since I had just ten months remaining on my enlistment, I would be assigned to the statistical services office at Sheppard, and not permitted to teach. When I asked what was needed to do the assignment, I was told that I needed to extend my enlistment to a year. I offered to take a short discharge and re-enlist for six years, but that would have been too much paperwork, so the personnel people insisted on the two-month extension.

A Changed Life

The Air Force gave me six weeks of instructor training and threw me into a classroom to teach people how to program the UNIVAC 1050, the computer which would be used for the Air Force's first automated supply system. I taught for a year, during which I double-shifted—taught a shift and went to school a shift to cram just as much knowledge as I could into my head. My future and the future of my family were now at stake. I'd begun my ultimate career a decade late; I needed to make up time.

In August of 1965, an important decision had to be made. Should I reenlist and complete the second half of what had been a lackluster career, or should I take the outstanding offer from the Caterpillar Tractor Company to do software maintenance and to develop an in-house data processing training program? Tough choice. Low four figures for the USAF. High four figures for Cat. School, school, and more school. When I left Cat four years later to do the same for a company in my native New England, Cat had a good in-house training program. I'd built it.

Passion In Search Of Purpose

The fire had been built. The passion was now in place and I sought the underpinnings, the foundation for what I was supposed to know to do what I'd been successfully doing all along. I picked up several degrees. A series of assignments took me into management, consultancy, and college teaching, and ultimately on the staff of a Board of Education.

Then something happened. In 1977, I'd written a book—a preparation manual for a computer test—and the publisher wanted it updated. I then became a freelance writer, still teaching in industry, and still doing some college teaching. In 1980, I began to write not only the book but also some feature articles for the computer trade press. In the following eight years, I would produce three-dozen books.

And The World Changed

In 1982, IBM released the Personal Computer, and my life hasn't been the same since. By 1984, that led me back into college teaching full time, followed by further education for a Master's Degree in Education. Then I again took the Strong's Vocational Interest Blank, the test I'd taken in high school thirty years earlier. This time the test had been refined—not only should I have *been* a teacher, I was best suited to be a teacher of adults.

I still do a little teaching—of adults. I do considerable writing, for anyone who's interested. Mechanical inabilities notwithstanding, there is a house on an island in a lake in Massachusetts that I built with my tools and hands. I dug the foundation hole. I poured the concrete. I laid the floor, the walls, and the roof. Put in the plumbing and septic. Wired it for electricity. Dug a well and put in a pump. And lived in it. No guidance counselor was going to tell *me* that I couldn't do what I'd decided to do.

Looking Back

At the head of the chapter, I asked:

How do you define ambition? From the retrospect of years of trying to avoid what my heart told me I should do, I would have to say that ambition is the impetus necessary to accomplish anything important in your life. I've been successful in nearly everything I have done—except one. I could not stay with one organization long enough to derive a retirement for conformity. I have had a message for the world, and in every part of my life I have sought to spread that message. I would like to think that there are many people whose lives are better because we came in contact.

Just what does ambition mean? Ambition means taking the steps to accomplish something worthwhile and sticking to it until you have accomplished it. I wish in my younger life I'd had a mentor who could have steered me into establishing goals and formulating plans to meet those goals. I would never have accomplished anything in my adult life had I not encountered an author named Robert Mager, whose book *Defining Educational Objectives* was a transformation in my intellectual life. Much of my life was turned backwards. I'd built one tremendous automobile to travel in long before I had any idea about where I'd like to travel. I hope that explanation is not obtuse. Want to build an ambition? Build a good set of goals first, then get out and get the underpinnings you need to make it happen.

How can you tell if you have ambition? Do you dream? Do you lie awake evaluating your options? Do you picture yourself in another scenario? Is there a strong interest that you think you'd like to pursue but have found reasons and excuses to avoid? How often do you hear of old men who go back and get a college degree? Or old women who take a sky dive? What has interested you from childhood? From the time my brother could pick up a pencil he wanted to be an artist. Today he is a successful commercial artist. How blessed I would have been had someone discovered the intellectual tools I had and the teaching interests I exhibited at a when young. It took me twenty-five years to find them.

How will you approach your ambitions? You'll get every bit of training you can find. You'll read everything you can locate about the subject. You'll find someone who can tutor you. Someone who can mentor you. Someone who can encourage you. We often are so entangled that the dream dangles and goes unfulfilled. By the time I finally got a fire under my butt, I had a wife, two kids, two automobiles, and a mortgage. That's not the easiest place to start. To pursue your ambition from there requires some sacrifice from everything and everybody. Consider the sacrifice needed for the long-term training for a doctor or lawyer.

How will you know you have realized your ambition? There may be accolades along the way. Items to hang on the wall. Honors given. The reward comes when you look yourself in the mirror every morning and are pleased with what you see. It comes when someone whose life you have touched credits the influence you have given.

Like Tevye in *Fiddler on the Roof*, I often ask God: "Would it spoil some great celestial plan if I were a wealthy man?" I had my chance at that—had I not collapsed in 1999, two months later my rented property and my business would have been bought by Walgreens, who bought a city block and all the businesses therein. But the same God who spared my life wasn't willing for me to retire and go away. He still has work for me to do. There are people whose lives I yet need to touch; perhaps somebody reading this book.

Ambition is the grease of the wheels of life. It's the "Up and at 'em" and don't even think of quitting until you have made it to where you want to be, where the satisfactions from doing it have outstripped the work it's taken to get there.

Chapter 7: Breaking Through the Brick Wall

Have you ever noticed that no matter what you wish to do, you must do something else first? It seems a perverse law of nature to find impediments to our ambitions. While our ambitions may be few, impediments to accomplish them abound. Let's take a few and see what can be said about them. There is no significance to the sequence given:

Indecision

Do you remember the song? "First you say you will and then you won't. You're undecided now, so what are you gonna do?" Whenever you select a direction for your life, accomplishment of anything supporting that direction requires focus. Indecision is the death knell of focus. Far better to begin something, correct the mistakes, and adjust the direction than to waffle endlessly, never deciding. The question is never "If I do *A* or if I do *B*." The result is that you do nothing. St. Paul told his followers "I would that thou were hot or cold."

Complaining

It doesn't even have to be our complaining. Complaints of any kind from any source sap your strength, make you tired, and discourage you from any important accomplishment. Better to avoid and ignore the complaints than to expend your resources to meet (or further) the complaints. Distinguish between legitimate concerns, which you should handle, and the harping and tearing of nerves brought on by frequent complaints.

Fear

Fear is a complaint that never passes your lips. It's a complaint lodged by your brain against your motivations in sufficient strength to have a debilitating influence. It's an internal influence over an external direction, placed there by someone who or something that you'll allow to have control over your life. The defeat of fear removes inhibitions and opens the pathway to potential successes.

Worry

Worry is fear conjured up in expectation of failure. There you can file your insecurities long before you have any need for them. Often a worry is without foundation. It's something over which you have little or no control anyway. Might as well file it under *Not Applicable* and control what you can control.

Regret

It's a reflection on the past; our perception of a mistake over which we can now exert no influence. The single benefit of a regret is our resolution that under the same set of conditions, the action we will take will vary.

Obstacles

Lack of money is always an obstacle. Lack of cooperation is another. A third is lack of time—but that is a controllable obstacle. Rules that somebody else imposes on us are also obstacles. One of the functions of a civilized society is that obstacles are placed before us, and we frequently have no control over them. Fences, warnings, traffic lights, and stop signs are obstacles we accept because we believe they provide a degree of safety.

Other obstacles, such as provided by petty bureaucracies are often avoidable either through contest or removing one's self from their influences. Lack of money is an obstacle that merely delays, but does not remove, the goal. Lack of cooperation takes either the location of other cooperation or the assumption of personal responsibility. The point is that few obstacles are dead ends. Going over, under, around, or through are always solutions, once you have determined that the goal is a worthy and necessary goal.

The Past Is Prologue

You can't undo it. You can merely learn from it. You can resolve not to repeat it. Often it may be necessary to bury it. Or it may be necessary to accommodate it. Refer to Unforgiveness, ahead.

Alibis and Excuses

We deceive ourselves. We are further addicted to allowing others to deceive us. Alibis, the attempt to remove the responsibilities we have undertaken, become reasons for accepting failures before they have happened. Excuses are the accommodations we make with the inconveniences of our lives, and our choices are to accept them and try to recover our actions or reject them and bypass the situation that brought them on. Accepting the alibi of another person is merely the first step before having to accept the responsibility of that person, allowing him or her to duck personal responsibility. Excuses may be valid with proper notification—but invalid when no advance communication has been made.

Tradition

"We've always done it this way" is by far the greatest explanation for failure to take new approaches, make changes, and to seek success in another direction. In 1993, I began to build my Avon business by opening a pair of retail stores. You can imagine how often I heard that I was violating the hundred-plus year tradition of Avon. By 1999, I was under pressure from Avon to shut them down. In 2007, Avon dealers began opening retail stores. What a difference a decade made. A pioneer is the one with all the arrows in his back. Note in 2018: the representative-in-a-store movement continued. Avon, on the other hand, is struggling and has responded as most large corporations do—by rolling heads. The corporation has been sold to a UK management company.

Envy

Wanting what anyone else has without the willingness to undergo what the other person has done to get it is envy. We are not all blessed by having the same talents, the same motivations, or the same effectiveness. We make different decisions. It's insufficient to look at another's accomplishments and merely wish those were ours. Time. Money. Effort. Sacrifice. They are all needed. Walking a mile in another's shoes is needed for success.

Criticism

For everything you'd like to do, there is always somebody whose primary focus in life is finding fault with it. They aren't willing to take the risk themselves, but are willing to find fault in the way you have done it. The best example I can offer is the one where I began to share some beauty tips from an industry expert. I was roundly criticized because her advice didn't line up perfectly with Avon's. When I challenged the critic to do it herself, her response was for me to copy Avon's materials. I rejected that. Had it been sufficiently important to me, I would have persisted. Those who agree with what you do are often silent, while those who would never think at putting themselves or their accomplishments at risk are quick to be critical. Something learned in my seventy-plus years: if you spend your time being critical of what somebody else does, you'll never get anything important done yourself.

Wrong Friends

Negativity is a popular bandwagon to ride. Every negative friend should be challenged, and if he or she fails to answer the challenge, you must re-evaluate the long-term benefits of the friendship. People can be categorized. Do you wish to associate with people whose interests don't support yours? If you do, be prepared for your ambitions to be denigrated and your efforts to be discouraged.

Supporting friends and colleagues can assist your efforts to success. You'd be wise to associate with them and forgo any association with what former Vice President Spiro Agnew termed "the nattering nabobs of negativity."

Mistakes

You'll make them. Everyone does. Mistakes are signposts to the future. Few of them are disastrous. Most tasks can be corrected and repeated. Many can be corrected over time by modifying approaches and actions. Only safety-oriented tasks require extraordinary advanced thinking and training—such as the handling of dynamite or switches on punch presses that mandate the use of both hands, separated from the crushing dangers of the machine. Sometimes we don't think through a situation in advance, often with tragic results.

There need be no life/death gamble. We may buy too much or too little merchandise. We may sell it at a profit or a loss. We learn what to do and what not to do, and further learn that expansions of our opportunities are to be taken in small, reasonably safe steps.

Unforgiveness

Resentment is the aftermath of envy or distasteful experience. If we're ever to penetrate this wall, we must learn to forgive the transgressions of others who, after all, are trying to operate in their best self-interest. A harbored grudge saps your strength in ways that are not obvious, but creates bitterness and occupies precious time, time that could be spent moving your agenda forward. The danger with unforgiveness is that it becomes a dowry for a future business marriage, a competition prize for the unaware aspirant, and the most difficult anchor you will ever attempt to raise.

Procrastination

The "round tuit" is an old joke, but the waste of the irreplaceable resource of time is a sadly-paid expense and is harmful to your forward progress. The opposite is not necessarily *hard charging*, but one must learn that there are two kinds of activity: those that you cannot avoid, like the work on taxes, which I'll start when I've said my piece here, and those which might be nice to do but never will get done if you don't get 'round tuit.' Procrastination is not slothfulness—but they are close relatives. Watch out.

Distractions

How often do we let TV, sports games, parties, alternative activities, and other choices dictate what we do? I marvel at people who can keep two, three, or four at-home businesses working. Working for more than one master means that you'll be doing far less than your best at any one. The best illustration I can give is a radio antenna—a vertically polarized antenna radiates equally poorly in all directions. A horizontally polarized antenna focuses all its energy forcefully in a single direction.

Lying

Without moralizing on what we tell others or what they tell us, it's fair to say that we frequently lie to ourselves. We say there is sufficient time, when we know there isn't. We say we have enough money, when we know we don't. We say we have planned when we know we have not. We say we can impose on the goodwill of others, when it's presumptuous to do so.

Lying is the lack of acceptance of personal responsibility, and you can assume that if these people ever become successful, they will have hit the lottery— one chance in 100 million or more.

Quitting

How easy to quit! Do nothing! Make excuses for our lack of performance. It's obvious to say that quitting is the antithesis of perseverance. Quitting in the face of an overwhelming challenge is strictly a character issue. You either have it or you don't. A significant part of self-motivbation is resolving to see something through.

There is a problem with quitting: you may be able to excuse it in others' eyes, but you cannot possibly excuse it in yours. If what you have quit is significant—especially if it's something that someone else is doing successfully—you'll always harbor that tinge of regret. You may well convince everybody other than yourself that you're not a quitter, but in the late night, in the early morning, and even in your dreams, the thought will haunt you. I guarantee it.

Double-mindedness

Play it safe. See if anybody will buy from you before you commit to sell something. Take on two businesses, should one not work. There is a time to take on more than you can chew—when you have so organized what you are doing that you can afford someone to assist you. Attempting one or more new tasks simultaneously, and justifying that they are complementary, is abject folly. Greater men than I have said that no man can serve two masters. The thought is not new. A prime self-motivator is singleness of purpose—specific and clear not only to you but also to those who would observe or follow you.

Hesitation

Lead, follow, or get out of the way. Ever sat behind a driver who was reluctant to enter the highway? After all, a car is coming—a couple blocks away. "Strike while the iron is hot," we are told. Good advice if you're a blacksmith. Hesitation for caution or complete evaluation is always wise. Hesitation for uncertainty is seldom wise. Learn to assess a situation by gathering the facts and evaluating them, then decide. Don't wait until everything is perfect. It will never happen. If you wait, somebody willing to avoid studying the situation to death will garner the reward. On the plains of hesitation line the bones of those who, with victory in their grasp, paused to rest.

Talking

"Happy talk, keep talking happy talk…" goes the song. " You got to have a dream; if you don't have a dream, how you gonna make a dream come true?" Talk to yourself. Tell yourself *positive* things. If you dwell on what is not to your liking, you drag yours motivation down. Things never will be precisely to your liking. If you're in business with an organization, that organization sets the rules under which you'll operate. If you don't like the rules, avoid that organization.

Rules change according to conditions. Then it becomes necessary to decide which rules you can accommodate and which you cannot. Often, a rule that you think you cannot accommodate steps on your emotional toes. You must decide whether a change in the circumstances is so sufficient to decide to *chuck it all*. Something we know—keep harping to yourself about the negatives and you bring unhappiness to your existence.

Look for the silver lining—and give yourself—and others—happy talk.

Failures

Everybody has them. Sometimes we get our feelings hurt. Other times we suffer extraordinary financial difficulty. The books are full of illustrations about people who have failed repeatedly, yet continue to pursue the dream until they have success. Read that sentence again—especially the phrase *until they have success*. There will be times when you make stupid mistakes. You're not alone. There will be times when you, in retrospect, will wish you had selected an alternate course.

You've heard: "If life hands you lemons, make lemonade." It's easy enough to feel frustrated when things don't go our way. To use a simple illustration, consider the difference in the traffic in your city on a Sunday morning to the rush-hour traffic of any weekday. Each of us has a plan to follow. Often times that plan comes into conflict with others' plans for themselves. So what? "Pick yourself up, dust yourself off, and start all over again."

Delay and Impatience

We're not a patient lot. We have a desire for instant gratification. It's a selfish impulse. That often means that we have little, if any, ability to plan beyond the ends of our noses. If we are to be successful, it will be because we have taken the time to plan our activities and have built into our plan sufficient space and time to accommodate the needs of others—our companies, our customers, and yes, even the demands on us. If planning is not done, crisis becomes our acquaintance, if not our friend, and becomes an easy enemy. If such planning is not done, over time everything becomes important. When that happens, many things can occur that will force us to take stock, stop and rest, and re-plan. The danger lies when we interpret crisis as the signal to quit, rather than the signal to take stock and re-plan.

Jealousy

Such a barrier! You find it whenever you feel you have come out on the short end of a bargain, when you should respect the bargaining process and recognize that in any bargain the validity of the transaction lies in the satisfaction of both parties, not merely one. Envy, while it's the desire for what someone has, can lead to jealousy merely because someone has something you don't.

To objectively overcome jealousy one must evaluate how another gained status, accomplishment, advantage, or reward—and if the outcome is important, to find ways not only to duplicate the actions that produced that gain, but also to exceed those gains. It's beating someone at his—or her—own game. Jealousy is a deleterious activity that can bog down any forward progress. Get rid of it and replace it with resolve.

Aimlessness

I find aimlessness in so many people who have made no efforts to set goals and plans to meet those goals. If you don't know where you are going, any direction will do. In business, aimlessness occurs when the person is willing to accept less than his or her potential and wishes to take the easy road. Robert Frost had it right when he said that he preferred to take the road less traveled. The road less traveled is the one that leads to success.

Nobody ever achieved success by merely copying the actions of another. Life is full of also-rans, people whose idea of success is *enough*. I've heard it so many times. "I have enough customers." Or "I work hard enough." Or "People ought to want to give me orders." To the self-motivated person there is never enough. There is always another customer. There is always another call to be made. There is always another product to be introduced.

Become satisfied with your efforts and next week you'll become satisfied with less effort, and over time you'll become less ambitious. If that happens, you'll determine that "this won't work for me." It won't work for you—until you build the fire under your butt and get moving again.

Disobedience, Strife, Misdirection, Conformity, Dishonesty, Ingratitude, Insecurity, and Lukewarmness are all parts of the balance of the fences you can erect. Companies make rules. You may not like the rules, and you should find a company whose rules you like. It probably won't happen. The natural tendency is to accept the rules you like and to reject those you don't. This leads to difficulties between you and your company, and the strife will wear on you.

In your frustration, you'll cast about in other directions, telling yourself and the world that you won't conform to the requirements placed on you. This may evidence itself in cheating—claiming returns that never occur, claiming non-receipt of product that was delivered. A downward spiral has begun and the thankfulness and joy of your early days goes out the window. You'll stick your thumb in your mouth and grab your security blanket, figuratively at least. From now on, you'll be ambivalent towards your company—lukewarm.

Break out of it. Self-motivation begins when you identify all those walls that confront you and resolve to surmount them, one by one, until victory is assured. Victory is possible, you know. The victory you seek.

Reward. Accomplishment. Self-satisfaction in your performance. Courage in the face of frustration. Resolve, when things get tough. Determination to overcome.

Chapter 8: Then What Should I Do?

For seven chapters now we have handled contributions to your self-motivation:

The Fear of Success

We offered that one way to become self-motivated is to overcome this *specific* fear. In it were outlined the items that impede our progress towards finding the success we were meant to have. The final message of that chapter acknowledged that if you'll put yourself in charge, all the other parts of success would fall into place.

Fear and Taking Risks

Recognizing that fear of success is but one of the fears we encounter, it was offered that fear is merely the reluctance to take risks. One by one some of the fears that you'll encounter are identified and approaches to those risks are offered.

Going Out On a Limb

Continuing the theme of handling risks—and by now you should be aware that success comes from the management of risk—you were charged to take responsibility for your risks and the chapter offered important attitudinal thoughts for your self-motivation.

Ambivalence to Ambition to Action

Here some techniques for moving from a position of "I don't care" to a position of "I care *very* much and here's what I'm going to do about it" were presented, with an exhortation to delay no further.

Preparing the Action Plan

Here we talked about solid actions you can take to ensure that your success does happen. Repetitive motivation has been covered here. This chapter will provide the stiffening of your backbone necessary to ensure that success.

Greasing the Wheels

Here we explored ambitions. We asked for definitions, and followed the path from the spark of an idea through the circumstances one finds oneself in, to the realization of an ambition.

Recognizing that people's circumstances differ, we

identified, with a chapter about breaking through the brick wall, the various impediments to fulfilling your ambitions. If we can identify and overcome those impediments, success is ours to claim.

Positive Self-Motivation

The following outlines a program of positive self-motivation that, if followed, could lead to outstanding results. Note that I have not said it *will* lead to success. These are *what* to do.

Unfortunately, human as we are, no little pill can be swallowed to obtain that fire in the belly. There is no choice but to develop a program and follow it religiously. If it's necessary to define the term *religiously*, merely draw to your attention that a religion consumes your life. Not that there are no other important aspects of your life. There are. A successful career becomes the enabler of an improved life in that it provides for all the other important features.

It's Not Complex

Living a self-motivated life is not difficult. There may be variations on the theme, but I maintain that to be self-motivated requires merely three steps, what I like to call attitude, fortitude, and vicissitude. Don't let that last word throw you. It's merely means circumstances.

"I'm gonna live 'til I die. I'm gonna reach for the sky. Before my number's up, I'm gonna fill my cup. I'm gonna live, Live, LIVE … until I die!" For those of you not fortunate enough to remember Broadway singer Ethel Merman, this song was her watchword—the religion of self-motivation she followed all her life. For an outstanding bit of motivational reading, I can highly recommend her biography, Ethel. If you do read it, you'll come away with an important message—Ethel Merman *believed in herself.* She was so certain of her worth and her capabilities that she inserted herself into every opportunity which either (1) befell her or (2) she created.

Again, the Attitude

I am convinced that the first step to a positive attitude is to believe in yourself. *Develop your faith in your abilities.* Adopt a reasonable confidence in your power. Overcome any sense of personal inferiority—no matter whether you tell that to yourself or you allow someone else to say it to you. Once you begin to believe in yourself, you'll unleash extraordinary inner powers that will manifest themselves in your outward positive actions. Once that happens, you'll have justified your faith in yourself. You have only to put the process into motion.

Following that thought one step further: *Never tackle merely something you know you can do.* Confidence never improves if you don't bite off a little more than you know you can chew. Nobody is suggesting you go over your head—but if you move cautiously from a zone of safety, you'll find that's where the growth is.

Go back and look at the lyrics of Ethel's song. What attitude shines through the song? First, and most important, is the idea of optimism. Listen again to Ethel: "You got to accentuate the positive; eliminate the negative; latch on to the affirmative. Don't mess with Mr. In-between."

Is attitude the attribute of happiness? Yes, it's that, but it's far more. It's enthusiasm, joy, expectation, curiosity, and preparation. It's telling yourself—and believing—that there will be a positive outcome from your efforts, and finding that positive outcome every time you go looking for it.

Personal satisfaction; Ethel Merman again: "I got plenty of nothin' and nothin's plenty for me." Well, I wouldn't go that far. The concept of self-motivation is that you shouldn't be satisfied with what you have thus far achieved. There is always another customer to see, another sale to make, and another bell to ring. Ambition begets achievement, which in turn promotes growth in your economics, in your influence, and in your results.

Determination

Doing the best job you can is an honor. It takes courage to achieve—what we like to call intestinal fortitude. It takes an attitude of unwillingness to accept failure easily, of unwillingness to let an issue die. You have a personal stake in the enterprise. Your challenge is to take it to the next step.

Adopt the position that you'll not allow yourself to fail. Don't accept the finality of the first "no" you hear. Or the second. Or the third. Tomorrow the answer may be "yes." For every "no" you hear, develop a reference. Somebody your "no" knows may well say "yes."

Develop another mantra: "I didn't get involved to go home a loser." Pick a strategy and try it. If it works, stick to it and build on your success. Take advantage of success. Plan for it. Success is the greatest bootstrap to the next level. Success is where the rewards are—and the direction in which your confidence will improve. Make sure you have a goal and the courage to try an untried strategy. Who knows? It might just work. Look for opportunities to exercise your entrepreneurial ingenuity.

Go With Your Cannons Loaded

You are an entrepreneur. If you have selected something you love to do, you'll never be affected by burnout. Your ladder reaches to the heavens and beyond. There is always another step to climb. Never allow yourself to rest on one rung long enough for boredom to tighten its grip. Be pleased with your success but always hungry for more. When the day finally arrives when no new challenges seem ready to present themselves, then go out and find some. Or create them. Be too busy to be bored. Closed doors don't discourage entrepreneurs. They either bang them down or build others. Or find windows to climb through.

If you were working for somebody else, would you wait until somebody decided you were worthy of promotion? If that were true, you might never advance, as you'd be perceived to lack any positive aggression. What would you do then? You'd ask for a raise. Why is that different because you're in business for yourself? From where does a raise come to you? From more business. From new customers. From larger orders. Why do you want more business? To get a raise! How will you tell your customers you deserve a raise? You do it by casting a brilliant spotlight on your achievements. You do it by letting your customers know—and demonstrating the truth of your statements—that you are the absolute *best*. You do it by demonstrating that there is *nobody* better than you.

If it's necessary to surmount your circumstances—do it. You *can* be better than the pressures placed on you. If it's necessary to invoke the higher power in your life, use all the help you can get.

What Is Your USP?

It's called a USP—a unique selling proposition. What do you offer that nobody else offers? Make your venture outstanding and positive. Key word, that: positive. That does *not* mean to give the store away. No one expects you to lose money, though they may attempt to get you to give away your profit.

Upswings and downswings: greet a downward turn with your best face. Can't undercut your competitor's prices? Outperform him with hard work and service.

Fully commit to the one organization that touches your heart. Put pressure on yourself. Answer this question: Are you *making* time or are you *marking* time? Be a self-starter. Be unafraid to shake up the status quo. Have courage. Force yourself into a no withdraw, no retreat position. Once you are there you'll have to do what it takes to advance—because you must never allow yourself to retreat.

Giving It What It Takes

Consider these statements:

- Necessities are easy to sell. All I need to do is to discover what is necessary for my customer. It's the way to find new customers. My service and my products fulfill personal needs.

- I'll just not be denied. Only my death will defeat me. I plan to be around a long time.

- I'll relish the unknown. The darkness of the unknown is but a thin disguise for a world ablaze with opportunity.

- I'll be an activist. I won't wait for someone to bring the market to me. I'll get out and find it.

- I'll make high demands on me. Nobody but I will do that. I'll know how I measure to myself. Everybody will know when I have successfully done it.

- I'll make a commitment to excellence. Not the usual. Not the also-ran. The best I can be. In the best way I know how.

- I'll find ways to bring my business to its fullest potential. Whenever I recognize that more potential exists, I'll seek a way to exploit it.

- I'll offer a necessary service. My customers will need me. I'll become indispensable to their needs.

- I love it. I rejoice in the course I have chosen to follow. I'll share that love and perhaps teach others to love it.

- I'm good at it. Nobody is better than I. I am the most successful person I know, and I'm going to improve on that wherever I can.

- I'll do something that has never been done, has seldom been done, or has not been done successfully by somebody else.

- I'll pressure me to outdo myself. Challenge sparks my engine.

- Once I've begun, I'll strive to be best, else I would allow someone to copy me and do it better.

- Somebody in front of me stopped. I'll "put the pedal to the metal," and cover that distance quickly.

- I'll find a vacuum and fill it. Nobody can fill it better than I. I'll be the first to find, so nobody else can exploit the opportunity.

- I'll see the possibilities where others see the liabilities.

- I'll keep a ledger of calls, one that identifies the hits and misses. Then I'll apply what I learned with the misses to increase the number of hits.

- I'll build an entrepreneurial resilience. Setbacks will be temporary. New strategies will be selected. I'll regroup and move ahead.

- I'll paint the vista. My customers will see the entire picture because I'll share it with them.

- However my business is going, there is always another bell to ring.

- I'll surmount my circumstances and my environment.

- I'll take full responsibility for the accomplishment of my success.

Pick your path to excellence and polish your crown. The only person who can fire you is yourself. Your business is your store. You close when you want to close. Business is always open. There are no ceilings. To move up, you must get recognition for your efforts. Look at us—we recognize one another—but we never tell the customer about it. Success comes from proving something can be done well and on your terms.

How Thin Is The Darkness?

The darkness of the unknown is a thin disguise for a world ablaze with opportunity. The fire in the belly, properly applied, eats at that darkness. The unknown becomes a thin veneer as you gain experience, confidence, and success.

Stop periodically and evaluate where you are and where you're going. As Sachel Paige once said, "Never look back. They may be gaining on you."

It's a vision thing. You'll move toward success when you perceive you *can* achieve outstanding success. In the movie Butch Cassidy and the Sundance Kid, Paul Newman (as Butch Cassidy) makes this statement: "I see visions while the rest of the world wears bifocals." You'll be successful because you *can* be successful. You can be successful because you know success lies in you. Your task lies in finding a way to coax it out. Set your goals majestically. Work toward accomplishment. Take the necessary steps, and you'll achieve. I guarantee it.

Passion Passes for Experience

I am absolutely convinced that the person with the leg up on persistence is the one who has that intense desire to succeed. Success is getting up one more day. Pursuing your dream one more day. It's taking the extra step. It's going beyond what anybody else will do. It's been said that there is no traffic jam on the extra mile.

You'll work hard, no doubt. If you're new at this, you'll work far harder than the "old pro's." If you do work that hard, you are entitled to, and will receive, the recognition for your efforts.

Build that desire this way:

Challenge your ability. Go after something that is beyond your ability with a strong desire to accomplish it. You'll do the work and you'll accomplish it.

Tell yourself that the limits you'll face today will be those you impose on yourself. No one can ruin your day without your permission. Life is full of people who didn't gain the prize on the first try, and worked daily to overcome limits on their performance.

Recognize that your advancement in your business and your rise in the ranks of your business will depend on your ability not to try to do something, but to complete it. Your competition has nothing on you.

Put pressure on yourself to develop your skills, overcome your fears, and accomplish your tasks. You must be the inspiration to yourself and to those who will choose to follow you.

Celebrate your achievements by accepting the

rewards and creating resolution to surpass your achievements. Build a plan and start this list again.

***

Napoleon Hill, in his book *Success Through a Positive Mental Attitude*, describes intense desire:

"Your subconscious mind begins to work under a universal law: what the mind can conceive and believe the mind can achieve. Because you realize your intended destination, your subconscious mind is affected by this self-suggestion. It goes to work to help you get there.

"Because you know what you want, there is a tendency for you to try to get on the right track and head in the right direction. You get into action.

"Work now becomes fun. You are motivated to pay the price. You budget your time and money. You study, think, and plan. The more you think about your goal, the more enthusiastic you become. With enthusiasm your desire turns into an intense desire.

"You become alerted to opportunities that will help you achieve your objective as they present themselves in your everyday experiences. Because you know what you want, you are more likely to recognize these opportunities."

What Is Great Performance?

It's a paradox that outstanding desire produces outstanding performance. The person with that level of desire, that passion, that *fire in the belly*, is not satisfied with *good* performance. He isn't interested in *average* performance. She has no desire to produce *acceptable* performance. That person is interested in and will accept nothing less than *great performance*, specifically as it applies to customers. Consider this set of questions:

Is this the best you can do? Are you doing the tasks in the best way you know they can be done?

What would you wish for your customers? Is it perfect service, no shorts, no foibles of human frailty, or no problems?

What do you feel your customers want? Is it reasonable to expect that in this sequence of human experience that the process will run with the precision of a fine Swiss watch? Or would a more reasonable and rational approach be a great performance?

How would you like your company to be run considering the best that *you* can do? Would you like it never to make a mistake? Would you like all shipments to be on time, without error, in perfect shape, and with no glitches?

It's useful to recognize here that our interest is in *great performance*, not in perfect performance. Perfection is ideal but attainable only to an extent. It's reasonable to ask what we *really* want to create for our customers and what it will take to make that happen. Great performance is largely a function of self-definition. Once I have decided to achieve great performance, nothing can deter that effort.

Burning desire is not something we can receive genetically from our parents. We can observe intense desire in someone else and model that behavior. Persistence is a trait that must be taught and assimilated. Again, we're not interested in the incrementalism of acceptable, typical, or good performance.

Thinking incrementally is something we're taught early in life. Parents, seeking to obtain great performance from their progeny urge them to try harder, take another step, and work a little more. They are taught the ranges for an A, B, C, and are encouraged to do the necessary steps to move from the lower range to the higher. Even in our professional lives we are given levels of performance to which our companies attempt to stir our aspirations.

Suppose the situation were turned around and those who showed intense desire and persistence were hired. What if we began with an extreme definition of great performance and worked backwards to identify the steps to get there? Suppose the idea is to produce on-time delivery of perfect product with no disruptions—would that get someone's attention? Perhaps the customers?

Now we know, as independent sales people, that it's *our* portion of the process over which we can exercise any control. We cannot do anything about our company's running out of product, except to pass the information back with carefully worded *suggestions* that they get with the program.

Your Pathway to Success

You must never give up if you know you're right. If getting into the business you have selected was right to do for the right reasons at the time of entry, it's no less right now. You have just to make your plans, commit to them, and get started, staying on task until you can see results.

You must believe that everything will work for you if you complete the process. There are so many instances in history—perhaps even your personal history—where had the course been stayed, the results would have been desirable. The abandonment of a worthwhile effort, even one with difficulty, merely allows one to make the same mistake repeatedly.

You must be courageous and unperturbed in the face

of difficulties. Tell yourself you'll fail and you'll fail. Tell yourself that despite any difficulties you might encounter, the goal is worthwhile and either way, you'll seek a means to accomplish that goal, and the aural reinforcement has such a way of permeating your psyche that you'll *find* a way to succeed.

You must not permit anyone—*anyone*—to deter you from your path or intimidate you to cause you to miss your goal. Many will tell you what you cannot do. Refuse to allow that to happen. It's *your* journey. You don't have to go it alone. That's what we're here for—those of us who share a journey not unlike yours. Positive and uplifting support is available to you 24/7 among those us on the same path.

You must fight to overcome all handicaps and setbacks. Sometimes this takes the form of the frustration of missing product. Sometimes it's irate customers. You, alone, control your mood. Fortify yourself with knowledge and understanding, skill and perseverance. Allow nobody to stand in your way. Nudge aside those who try to give them with severe warnings.

You must try repeatedly to accomplish what you desire. And again, if necessary. Persistence is: "No one could make that ram scram; he kept buttin' that dam." If I recall the song, the punch line was "Whoops, there goes a billion kilowatt dam."

Accept the fact that nobody you ever heard about, whoever accomplished anything significant, had it handed to her. She had to fight discouragement. She had to fight adversity. She suffered temporary failure and fought to recover. Success was in her sights, and though she may have had to fight to see it done, she'd done so—or is doing so currently.

Recognize that if you'll not surrender to discouragement or fear, or whatever obstacles may lie in your path, you'll achieve the goal.

If you are wise enough to establish your goals as short-term achievable steps, you'll find that success brings an emotional surge to your performance, further boosting your efforts.

Do Something Different

As you set goals, plan to do something novel. Take a bold move. Don't do things as you've always done them. Don't do them as others have always done them. As you make plans, plan something radical:

- Start selling in a nearby town that may not be well served.

- Place an ad in a newspaper where you never see an ad for your product.

- Find several helpers in several parts of town.

- Open an office and do your business from there.

- Get yourself into a training schedule.

- Be a friend to every representative you know—even your competition.

- If you've been buying 10 or 20 sales brochures, buy 100. Rent a kid to distribute them.

- Get yourself a bicycle and drag a wagon around.

- Pull your kids around in a little Red Wagon.

- Go to two businesses a week or more and give out books.

- Go to two doctor's offices a week or more and give out books.

- Stand a half hour in the parking lot at the grocery store handing out books.

- Find a five-story (or larger) office building and take the elevator to the top floor. Walk around giving out books. Walk down the stairs; do the same on each floor.

- Do you get the idea? Make it *different*. If you do the same as you've done before, you'll get the same results. Do something different. Better to attempt something new and big—and fail, than to attempt nothing—and succeed.

"I am not judged by the number of times I fail, but by the number of times I succeed. The number of times I succeed is in direct proportion to the number of times I can fail and keep on trying."

Motto of the Champions Unlimited, Scottsdale, AZ.

EPILOG

I have learned that business fear is a heavy burden. With faith, divine inspiration and intervention, a little luck, friends, acquaintances, and hard work, you can achieve more—and a different—success than your wildest imagination may ever have guessed.

At the same time, overcoming business fear is your crowning achievement. But nobody other than you will polish your crown.

Some years ago, I encountered the following, and I end the book the same way I begin it:

Be Different
Be Better
Be Successful

You Know
You Can!

###